CH

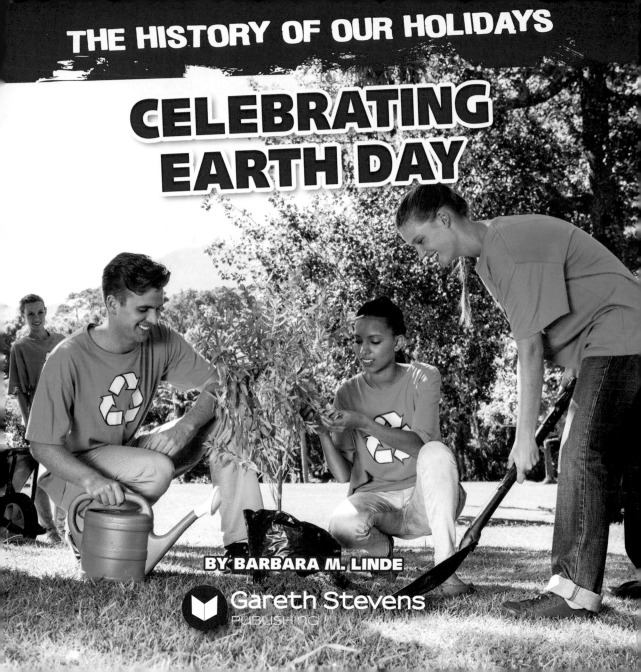

CELEBRATING EARTH DAY

BY BARBARA M. LINDE

Gareth Stevens
PUBLISHING

Please visit our website, www.garethstevens.com. For a free color catalog of all our high-quality books, call toll free 1-800-542-2595 or fax 1-877-542-2596.

Library of Congress Cataloging-in-Publication Data

Names: Linde, Barbara M.
Title: Celebrating Earth Day / Barbara M. Linde.
Description: New York : Gareth Stevens Publishing, 2020. | Series: The history of our holidays | Includes glossary and index.
Identifiers: ISBN 9781538238585 (pbk.) | ISBN 9781538238608 (library bound) | ISBN 9781538238592 (6 pack)
Subjects: LCSH: Earth Day–Juvenile literature. | Environmental protection–Juvenile literature. | Environmentalism–Juvenile literature.
Classification: LCC GE195.5 L57 2020 | DDC 394.262–dc23

Published in 2020 by
Gareth Stevens Publishing
111 East 14th Street, Suite 349
New York, NY 10003

Copyright © 2020 Gareth Stevens Publishing

Designer: Laura Bowen
Editor: Barbara M. Linde

Photo credits: Cover, pp. 1, 15 wavebreakmedia/Shutterstock.com; pp. 2–24 (background texture) secondcorner/Shutterstock.com; pp. 3–24 (background flags) saicle/Shutterstock.com; p. 5 Gene Daniels/US National Archives bot/Wikimedia Commons; pp. 7 (main), 9 Bettmann/Getty Images; p. 11 RAVEENDRAN/AFP/Getty Images; p. 13 Lori Adamski Peek/The Image Bank/Getty Images; p. 17 Vova Shevchuk/Shutterstock.com; p. 19 Ruslan Shugushev; p. 21 Steve Debenport/E+/Getty Images.

Printed in the United States of America

CPSIA compliance information: Batch #CS19GS: For further information contact Gareth Stevens, New York, New York at 1-800-542-2595

CONTENTS

Boldface words appear in the glossary.

Big Problems

Imagine bodies of water full of **poison**. Picture parks and other places full of trash. Think about dirty, smoky air. In 1970, our **environment** was in trouble. Many people and businesses didn't take good care of it.

5

A Senator Helps

Senator Gaylord Nelson knew about these problems. He wanted to help. He talked to other government leaders. He talked to business owners and **citizens**. Some people didn't listen, but others wanted to work with him. He planned the first Earth Day.

First Earth Day, New York City

The First Earth Day

The first Earth Day **celebration** was on April 22, 1970. All over the United States, people got together. They talked about cleaning up the land, air, and water. They asked the leaders to make new laws to help the environment.

Earth Day, 1970

What Happened Next?

Soon, laws about the environment were passed. People and businesses followed the new laws. The water, land, and air got cleaner. By 1990, other countries started Earth Day celebrations. Now, more than 190 countries celebrate Earth Day.

CONSERVE RAIN WA
BECAUSE EVERY
DROP COUNTS

TAP THE TAP
PUT A
STOP
THE DROP

AVE
WATE

Earth Day celebration, India

Earth Day Actions

Good things happen every Earth Day. Leaders talk about stopping **pollution**. People listen and take action. They plant new trees and take trash out of the water. They clean up parks and streets. Communities plan to ride bikes instead of driving cars.

A Green Day

Each Earth Day has a theme, or main idea. One year it was "Clean Earth–Green Earth." Leaders asked people to think about keeping the environment clean. That helps plants and trees grow better. Earth needs strong plants and trees to keep it healthy.

Goodbye, Plastic!

We often only use plastic straws and cups once. Then we throw them away. They float on the water or pile up on land. One year, Earth Day leaders asked people to stop using them. Many people agreed and stopped!

You Can Go Green!

You can celebrate the ideas of Earth Day every day! **Reduce** what you use. Turn off lights, computers, and TVs. Use less water to take a bath or to brush your teeth. Walk or bike to nearby places.

19

Reuse bottles and boxes. Take cloth bags when you shop. Give away old toys, books, and clothes instead of throwing them away. Use both sides of a piece of paper. **Recycle** cans, paper, and glass. You don't have to wait until the next Earth Day to ask your friends and family to join you, too!

GLOSSARY

celebration: a time to show happiness for an event through activities such as eating or playing music

citizen: a person who lives in a country legally and has certain rights

environment: the conditions that surround a living thing and affect the way it lives

poison: something that causes illness or death

pollution: harmful things that make the land, air, or water dirty or not safe to use

recycle: to treat something so it can be used again instead of throwing it away

reduce: to cut down on the amount of something

senator: a government leader from a state

BOOKS

Berne, Emma Carlson. *Earth Day*. North Mankato, MN: Cantata Learning, 2018.

McDonald, James. *I Am Earth: An Earth Day Book for Kids*. Salem, OR: House of Lore Publishing, 2016.

WEBSITES

Earth Day Facts for Kids
www.kids-world-travel-guide.com/earth-day.html
Read about the history of Earth Day and why Earth Day is important.

National Geographic Kids. Save the Earth!
kids.nationalgeographic.com/explore/celebrations/earth-day/#earth-day-cleanup.jpg
Find out about things children can do to help save the Earth.

INDEX